Respondir Traditional

GW01460252

Key Stage Two/Primary Four-Six

Contents

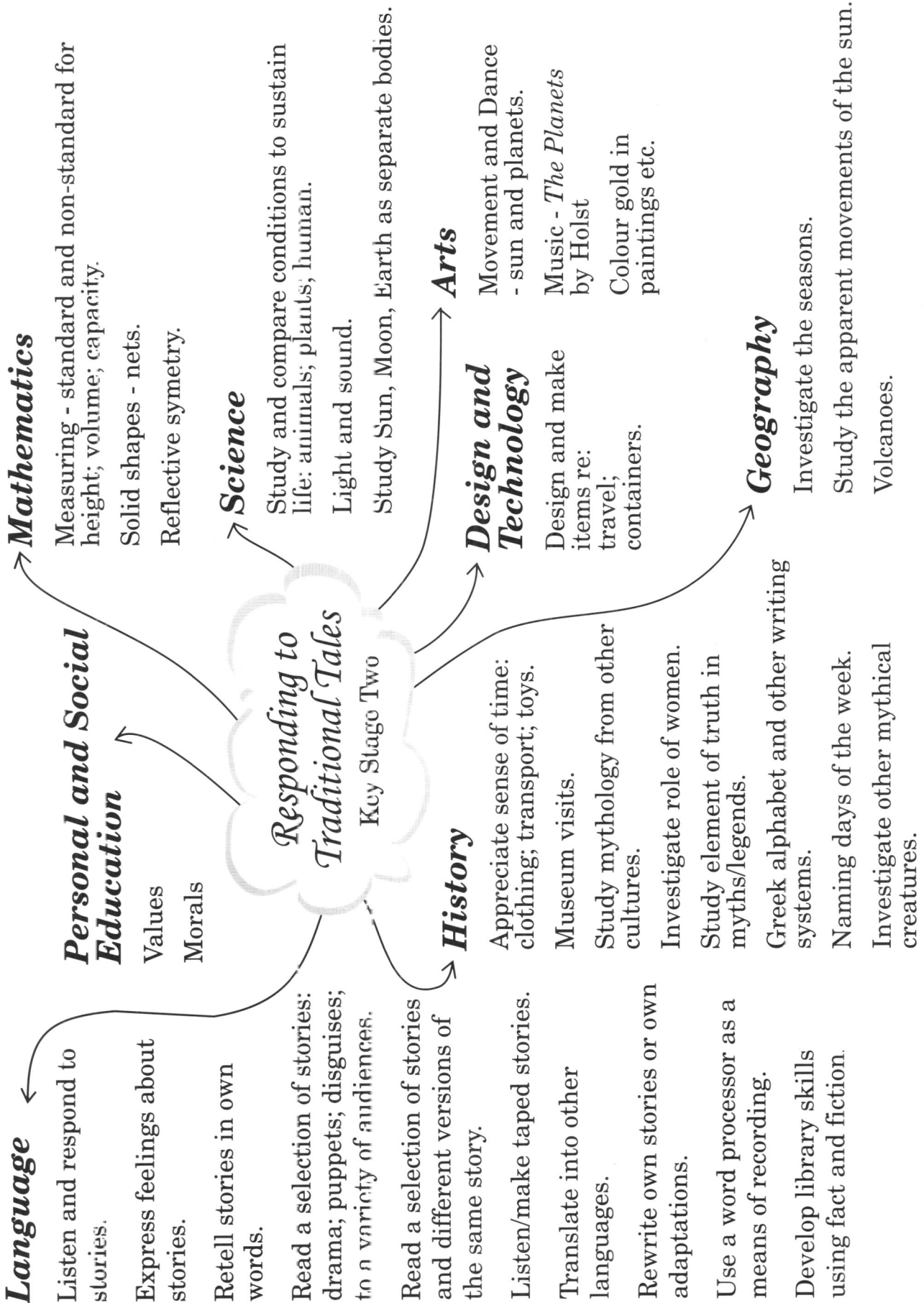

Topic Web

Responding to Traditional Tales — Key Stage Two

Mathematics

Measuring - standard and non-standard for height; volume; capacity.

Solid shapes - nets.

Reflective symetry.

Science

Study and compare conditions to sustain life: animals; plants; human.

Light and sound.

Study Sun, Moon, Earth as separate bodies.

Arts

Movement and Dance - sun and planets.

Music - *The Planets* by Holst

Colour gold in paintings etc.

Design and Technology

Design and make items re: travel; containers.

Geography

Investigate the seasons.

Study the apparent movements of the sun.

Volcanoes.

Personal and Social Education

Values

Morals

History

Appreciate sense of time: clothing; transport; toys.

Museum visits.

Study mythology from other cultures.

Investigate role of women.

Study element of truth in myths/legends.

Greek alphabet and other writing systems.

Naming days of the week.

Investigate other mythical creatures.

Language

Listen and respond to stories.

Express feelings about stories.

Retell stories in own words.

Read a selection of stories: drama; puppets; disguises; to a variety of audiences.

Read a selection of stories and different versions of the same story.

Listen/make taped stories.

Translate into other languages.

Rewrite own stories or own adaptations.

Use a word processor as a means of recording.

Develop library skills using fact and fiction.

Teachers' Notes

How to use this book

Responding to Traditional Tales Key Stage Two provides material for introducing children to the world of mythology in an interesting and meaning ful way. The selection of stories offers some insight into how people of the past tried to make sense of many aspects of the natural and supernatural world. Many words and sayings in the English language have derived from Greek mythology.

Some of the myths and legends chosen also involve moral dilemmas. When choosing which one to use with children it is important to be aware of the issues which may arise during follow-up discussions

The photocopiable sheets can be used in whole class situations or by individual children as appropriate.

This book is an ideal resource for teachers working with children on a short-term basis. Working with the myth or legend might last for half and hour, a day or even longer.

The *Teachers' Notes* on curriculum areas, in conjunction with the *Topic Web*, exemplify the possibilities of each myth or legend and should become evident for the particular group of children involved.

Getting started in the classroom

It is good practice to plan how and when you will introduce a new myth or legend to children.

It can be the centre of a scheme of work or integrated into other topics, for example *Robin Hood* when studying Trees or Wood or *The Chariot of the Sun* when studying Outer Space.

Allow plenty of time to introduce the story, read it to the children with appropriate pauses for comments and explanations if necessary and allow time for follow-up discussion.

It may be worthwhile reading the material more than once before moving on to the follow-up activities.

If the teacher is familiar with the story s/he will be able to prompt certain relevant questions if not forthcoming from the children, for example,

'Was Robin Hood right to have acted as he did?'

'Should Helios have allowed his son to have his own way?'

Even with a minimum of preparation, each story can lead to oral discussion and awareness of differing literary traditions.

Evaluation Sheets

The *Teacher's Checklist* can be used as an ongoing record of skills covered by individual children as the topic progresses. The information can then, if necessary, be transferred to a more formal record at a later date.

The *Pupil's Own Checklist* gives each child an opportunity to become more actively involved in her/his own recording of achievements. Depending on the child's ability, s/he may draw or write in the spaces provided. This also gives the teacher the opportunity to assess children's understanding of their own learning.

Areas Covered

(Refer to *Topic Web.*) These suggestions have been made with reference to the National Curriculum. They provide some introductory and follow-up activities which will enhance children's learning and enjoyment but are by no means exhaustive.

Language

Use an artefact or other visual aid to introduce some aspect of the story during its initial telling.

Try to have several copies and different versions of the same story available in the classroom. Draw the children's attention to the similarities and differences between texts and illustrations. Encourage them to say which they prefer and why.

Retelling the stories can be done in a variety of ways: dramatic play using simple costumes or masks; puppets; cut-out pictures on the magnet or felt board.

Children for whom English is their second language will probably benefit from greater clarification of the more complex stories. Retell them in the teacher's own words, use more visual aids or even arrange for the parents to translate into their first language.

Rewrite the stories in the children's own words by making their own books or plays. Use the word processor and provide a word bank of key words to assist them. Opportunities for collaborative writing, drafting and redrafting will emerge.

General punctuation, grammar and spelling patterns can be highlighted for the whole class, for example the use of speech marks; hood, wood and other spellings with the same sound such as should, could, would.

Explore antonyms (opposites), prefixes and suffixes (*Pandora's Box*).

Library skills can be extended whereby children retrieve more information related to their chosen topic. They will also need to differentiate between fact and fiction.

Work can be presented to a variety of audiences: a peer group; a younger class; an Assembly.

Mathematics

Estimating and confirming measurements of items mentioned in the myth or legend, for example the height of sunflowers could be recorded (Clytie). Further work could involve children measuring themselves.

The volume of various boxes could be estimated and then calculated (*Pandora's Box*).

Solid shapes and their nets could be investigated starting with the rectangular prism (*Pandora's Box*).

Symmetry (*Echo and Narcissus*) to explore reflections and balance. Rotational symmetry may be more appropriate for older children.

Science

Various elements of each myth or legend may be developed as mini-topics in themselves:

• Life study of animals involved in the stories such as spiders (*Arachne*).

• Conditions to sustain human life (*King Midas*), conditions to sustain plant life such as sunflowers (*Clytie*). Experiment with the controlled conditions of heat/light/moisture.

• A comparison of the three sets of conditions required for human, other animal and plant life could be undertaken.

• Reflections of light and sound (*Echo and Narcissus*) and further investigations into Colour and Light.

Design and Technology

Design, construct and modify where necessary models for Helios' chariot or Pandora's Box. The ideas could be extended to a jewellery box or gift box if more appropriate.

History

Through stories children can experience aspects of what it may have been like to live at the time of the story. The kinds of clothes, houses, toys or transport can be noted.

Discuss the characters, 'Are they real or imagined?' (*Robin Hood* or *Persephone*). 'What happened to them?' 'How much truth lies behind the legend or myth?'

Museum visits can extend the knowledge of particular cultures if studying mythology and legends from other cultures.

Investigate the role of women in history.

Introduce the Greek alphabet and other writing systems - Roman, Arabic, Ancient Egyptian hieroglyphs, etc.

How we named the days of the week (*Thor's Day*) can lead to origins of the names of the months.

Geography

Study the true facts about the seasons (Persephone) and other climatic patterns or cycles.

Investigate the apparent movement of the sun across the sky (*The Chariot of the Sun*).

Investigate volcanoes (Etna in *Persephone*).

The Arts

Music, movement and dance will be inspired by the theme of the Sun and the Planets (*Chariot of the Sun*). The music of The Planets suite by Holst could be useful. Make paintings and collages using the colour gold (*King Midas*).

Personal and Social Education

Ask questions about any moral issues involved, for example *King Midas* or *Robin Hood*. The differences between rights and wrongs lead to interesting discussions, for example *Pandora's Box*.

How do we value certain attributes or objects? (*King Midas*).

CLYTIE

CLYTIE was a very beautiful water nymph. She was in love with Apollo, god of the sun, but he did not return her love. Clytie sat all day upon the cold damp ground with her masses of golden tresses streaming over her shoulders. Nine days she sat and tasted neither food nor drink. Her own tears and the cold dew being her only food. She gazed at the sun as he rose in the east and watched him as he travelled across the sky to his palace in the west. She saw no one else for her eyes always followed him.

At last, they say, her limbs were rooted in the ground and her face became a flower: a flower which turns its head on its stem to follow the sun's daily course.

And so today, the sunflower turns on its stem to watch the sun and he rises in the east and travels across the sky to his palace in the west; for the sunflower still retains the feelings of Clytie.

Growing Sunflowers

NAME ....

Grow some sunflowers and see if the flower heads really do follow the sun throughout the day, like Clytie. Giant sunflower plants grow very fast and the flower can be as large as a dinner plate. See if any insects come near them.

What you need:

☆sunflower seeds   ☆tape measure   ☆notepaper and pencil

☆pots   ☆potting soil

The best time to plant the seeds is in Spring.

How to grow sunflowers:

Fill the pots with the potting soil or find a position in the garden which gets lots of sun. (Against a wall or a fence is a good spot.) Plant the seeds in the soil by pushing them down about 1 cm into the soil and about 60 cm apart so they have room to grow. Lightly water the seeds in. The seeds should be watered every day and shoots should appear after 10 to 12 days. Measure the growth of the sunflower each week and see who can grow the tallest sunflower.

Once the plants have finished flowering, collect the seeds from the flowers and put them in an envelope. Label and date the envelope and put it in a dry place until next year when you can then plant the seeds.

Sun Words

NAME ....

In the following word search there are many words which contain the word 'sun'. Colour in all the sun words that you can find. Most of these words are **compound** words which means that they are made up of two words, for example, sunlight.

Q	S	S	M	N	S	U	N	R	A	Y	O	H	D	L	Q	E	K	S	S
H	U	U	O	W	S	E	S	S	A	L	G	N	U	S	D	F	U	I	U
O	N	N	O	O	I	S	U	N	S	H	I	N	E	A	G	N	G	S	N
I	G	T	R	D	C	I	S	U	N	L	I	G	H	T	B	O	O	U	D
F	L	A	N	N	L	L	N	D	B	L	E	S	E	O	D	S	K	N	O
C	O	N	U	U	E	F	K	N	M	E	N	A	N	N	U	K	P	D	W
S	W	O	S	S	I	H	U	N	S	U	D	N	U	N	D	Y	S	I	N
U	U	L	R	S	F	S	T	I	S	N	E	S	L	H	A	A	U	A	E
N	S	N	H	N	U	I	R	A	U	T	C	I	G	P	B	D	N	L	R
P	E	N	B	F	U	N	L	S	B	D	T	K	K	S	U	N	S	E	T
R	I	R	I	I	U	S	D	S	U	N	G	L	A	S	S	U	T	B	N
O	R	U	S	S	R	R	M	R	O	S	U	N	L	E	S	S	O	J	O
O	D	B	U	N	S	D	E	H	E	P	F	S	B	U	R	D	N	M	E
F	N	N	N	S	P	U	T	W	M	S	U	H	N	M	C	B	E	E	N
C	U	U	L	H	U	S	N	A	O	N	S	B	H	T	A	B	N	U	S
L	S	S	O	F	A	N	L	B	B	L	O	T	A	H	N	U	S	U	B
I	I	H	U	F	B	N	D	E	A	W	F	J	S	U	N	D	R	Y	S
A	M	A	N	P	U	J	A	E	M	K	J	N	S	U	N	S	U	I	T
I	M	U	G	S	A	M	F	P	W	L	E	S	U	N	H	O	O	D	N
N	S	E	E	T	S	R	U	B	N	U	S	U	N	S	P	O	T	K	J

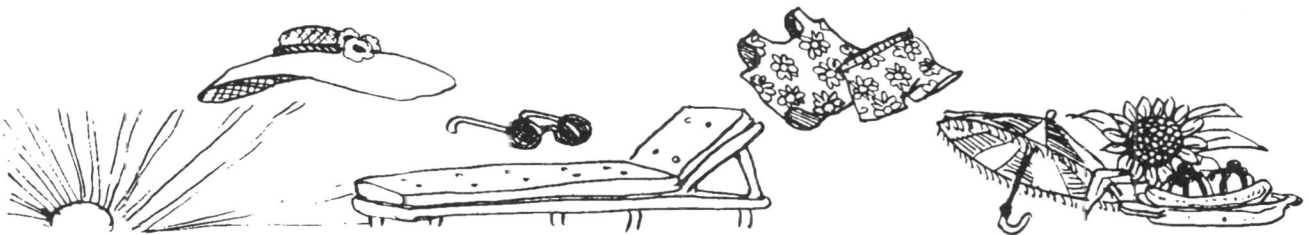

Robin Hood

*L**ONG** long ago there lived a man named Robin Hood. Robin Hood had many followers, called his merry men, and they all lived in the Sherwood Forest. There was Little John who was Robin's closest friend, Friar Tuck who loved his food and drink and was a very good fighter; and there was Alan-a-dale who was always happy to sing and play his mandolin. They had one enemy, the Sheriff of Nottingham, for they were outlaws and spent their days shooting with their bows and arrows. They could shoot better than anyone else in the land. It is said that they stole from the rich and gave to the poor.

One day, there was a shooting contest in the town of Nottingham which was near to the forest where the merry men lived. "Let's go to the contest," said Robin Hood. "We will be quite safe as no one will know who we really are." The winner of the contest was to receive a silver arrow. So the next day they all rode into Nottingham. The contest had already begun.

Now the Sheriff of Nottingham, an evil man who hated Robin Hood, was watching the contest. Robin Hood and all his men took turns at shooting and, of course, Robin Hood won. As he went up to the sheriff to collect his prize, someone cried out, "Hey, that's Robin Hood!" The sheriff jumped up and shouted, "Don't let him get away". The sheriff and his men chased the outlaws and shot at them. Little John was shot in the knee. "Leave me behind and go on," shouted Little John; but his friends would not and one of the outlaws carried Little John on his back.

The outlaws came to a castle which belonged to Richard, a friend of Robin Hood's. Robin knew that Little John needed help so he decided to enter the castle. Richard had seen the men approaching and lowered the drawbridge so that they could get inside. The drawbridge was then immediately raised so that the sheriff and his men could not get into the castle. The sheriff of Nottingham could do nothing but return to his town. Robin and his men rested in the castle before returning to their secret place in the forest. Little John remained in the castle until his knee had healed.

The sheriff was furious with Richard for allowing Robin and his men into the castle. He decided to lie in wait for Richard outside the castle. After some time, when Richard felt it was quite safe to go hunting, he left his castle and the sheriff's waiting men took him prisoner. Richard's wife went to Robin Hood and pleaded with him to help her get her husband back. Robin Hood called his men together at once and they all rode into Nottingham to fight the sheriff.

The people of Nottingham hid in their houses for they knew a battle was to be fought. A great fight was held in the streets until at last the sheriff of Nottingham was shot by Robin. Robin then freed Richard who went to live in the forest with Robin and his merry men.

Posters

Design a Wanted Poster for Robin Hood and one for the Sheriff of Nottingham. Use the following guide to collect information about these two characters before you make your poster.

Name: _____   _____

Description: _____   _____
_____   _____

Places where seen: _____   _____
_____   _____

Wanted for: _____   _____
_____   _____

Friends and associates: _____   _____
_____   _____

Enemies: _____   _____
_____   _____

Reward: _____   _____

Once you have collected all the information needed, create your posters on large sheets of paper and display them around the classroom.

Robin Hood Maze

NAME ....

Help Robin Hood to collect his friends and reach Sherwood Forest.
Begin with Robin and collect his friends in the following order:

Little John   Alan-a-dale   Friar Tuck

When you collect each friend, you must enter through one entrance and
leave by the other.

THOR'S DAY

T *HOR* was the son of Odin and very stong. He had fierce blue eyes and a bright red beard. Thor travelled in a brass chariot which was drawn by two goats. One goat was called Tooth-gnasher and the other was called Gap-tooth. Thunder rumbled whenever Thor travelled in his chariot across the sky. Thor lived in Asgard which was a beautiful place full of sunshine, singing birds and beautiful flowers. Thor defended Asgard against the Frost Giants who were always trying to get into Asgard. Thor was strong and had three magic helpers to help him defend Asgard. The first was a hammer. Whenever Thor threw the hammer it flew back to him. The second magic helper was his pair of magic gloves. These gloves helped Thor grab hold of the magic hammer. The third magic helper was a magic belt. When Thor put on his magic belt his strength doubled.

One morning, after a long sleep, Thor woke up and found that his hammer was missing. He searched everywhere but could not find it. He then became angry and called for Loki who often used to play tricks on the other gods. Loki told Thor that he thought Thrym the giant had stolen the hammer and so Thor flew to Giant's Land to ask him. Thyrm laughed and admitted that he had stolen the hammer and had hidden it deep in the earth where no one could ever find it. He said he would only return it if Freya, a beautiful goddess, would marry him. When Freya heard this, she cried and said that she would never marry such an ugly giant. The other gods did not want her to but said they must get the hammer back if Asgard was to be kept safe by Thor.

Loki then thought of a plan. Thor dressed up like a bride and went to Thrym, pretending to agree to marry him. Thrym was overjoyed when his bride arrived and prepared a huge feast for her and her bridesmaid (who was really Loki in disguise). At dinner the bride ate everything in sight: a whole ox, eight salmon and loads of vegetables and fruit. Thrym was very surprised that a woman could eat so much but the bride explained it was because she had been so excited that she had not eaten for a week. Thrym was delighted that she felt so strongly for him and lifted her veil, as gently as a giant could. He dropped the veil quickly when he saw her fierce blue eyes.

After the feast Thrym tried to kiss his bride but Loki said the wedding must be held first and that the hammer must be given to the bride as a wedding present. Thrym agreed, fetched the hammer and placed it on her knee. At that moment the bride tore off the veil and there stood Thor. He grabbed the hammer and swung it all around. The castle rocked; lightning flashed and thunder crashed all around. The castle fell in a heap to the ground, killing every giant in it.

And so Thor and Loki returned to Asgard and lived happily ever after, knowing that the giant was dead. Now we celebrate Thor's bravery every week on his day – Thursday.

Thor

Read the following sentences from the myth *Thor's Day* and draw a picture to show the god Thor and the place where he lived. Display your drawing around the classroom.

Thor was very strong and he had fierce blue eyes and a bright red beard. Thor travelled in a brass chariot which was drawn by two goats. One goat was called Tooth-gnasher and the other was called Gap-tooth. Thor lived in Asgard which was a beautiful place full of sunshine, singing birds and beautiful flowers. Thor was strong and had three magic helpers to help him defend Asgard. The first was a hammer. The second magic helper was his pair of magic gloves. The third magic helper was a magic belt.

Echo and Narcissus

*E*CHO was a lovely nymph who had a very beautiful voice. She was so fond of her voice that she rarely stopped talking. Juno, the queen of all gods, was very fond of this nymph and she too liked to hear Echo speak. But one day, when Juno asked Echo to be quiet, Echo was rude and so Juno punished her. "I am going to punish you," declared Juno. "You may keep your sweet voice, but you may only speak after someone else has spoken to you, and then you can only say the word that has just been said."

Poor Echo ran away in sorrow and hid herself in the hills. The other nymphs noticed that she spoke very little and only after they had spoken. Though she looked the same, they could scarcely believe that this sad nymph who wandered up the hills and down the valleys was the once bright and noisy Echo.

There was at that time a beautiful youth whose name was Narcissus. As he was wandering in the hills, Narcissus lost his way so he called out loudly, "Is there anybody here?" Echo was resting under a tree close by, looked out and at once fell in love with him. She called out, "Here." But, as he could see nobody, Narcissus called again, "Who are you?" "You," replied Echo, repeating his last word. As he could still see nobody Narcissus went on his way.

Just then, Echo felt her punishment more than ever, for she very much wanted to speak to the lovely boy and ask him to stay with her. But of course she could not call to him and so he disappeared out of sight. Full of sorrow, Echo sank down onto the grass and wept for her lost Narcissus. For days and days she remained in the same place till at last she faded away and only her voice was left. You may now hear it, wandering up hill and down dale, but speaking only after you have spoken and saying the same words as you have said.

Narcissus went on up into the mountains and soon he became thirsty and, coming to a clear pool, bent to take a drink from it. He saw in the pool an image and he fell in love with it. He did not know that it was his own image and asked, "Who are you?" "You," replied a voice, which was all that was left of poor Echo. Narcissus looked around but could see nobody. He smiled and, on looking again into the water, saw a pretty face smiling back at him. He put down his hand to try to touch it but, as soon as he touched the water, the ripples on the pool hid the image. When the water became still again, the lovely face was there looking up at him, smiling. The more he looked at it, the more he loved it.

He could not stop gazing into the pool. Days went by, but still he stayed there. Whenever he spoke, only his own words came back in reply, so he thought that the image was mocking him. He grew thin and weak, too weak to leave the side of the pool. At last he faded away altogether.

When his friends came to look for him, they found that a beautiful flower had sprung up where he had rested. They called it Narcissus, the name it still bears.

Echo and Narcissus

Below are twenty-one sentences about a part of the myth *Echo and Narcissus*. Rewrite these sentences in the order in which they occurred in the myth. You may like to make up a timeline to show when you think the events occurred. For example; in the morning, on a weekday, over a month, or even years.

Narcissus came to a pool in the mountains and bent to take a drink.

Echo ran away in sorrow and hid herself in the hills.

When the water was still, the lovely face smiled at him again.

He grew thin and weak; too weak to leave the pool.

As he could see nobody, he went on his way.

He could not stop gazing into the pool.

A beautiful youth named Narcissus, wandering in the hills, lost his way.

Echo was a lovely nymph who had a very beautiful voice.

His friends came looking for him and found a flower where he had rested.

The more he looked at it, the more he loved it.

Echo was rude to Juno and so Juno punished her.

For days she stayed in the same place till she faded away.

Juno, the queen of all gods, was very fond of this nymph.

He smiled and, looking into the water, saw a face smiling at him.

At last he faded away altogether.

Full of sorrow, Echo sank down onto the grass.

He touched the water but, as he touched it, the ripples hid the image.

She was so fond of her voice that she rarely stopped talking.

They called it Narcissus, the name it still bears.

Echo was resting under a tree close by and at once fell in love with him.

He saw his image in the pool and he fell in love with it.

Arachne

ARACHNE was a beautiful maiden and the best weaver that had ever lived. Nymphs came from miles around to see her beautiful work. Everyone agreed that only Athene, the goddess of Love, could have taught her. Arachne told everyone that no one had taught her but that she had taught herself. She even said that she would be glad to have a contest with Athene to see who was the better weaver. In vain her father told her that perhaps the goddess had guided her hand but Arachne would not listen and would thank no one for her great skill.

One day, as Arachne was boasting her skill, an old woman came to her and begged her to insult Athene no more. She warned her that no mortal could hope to become an equal of a god or goddess and invited her to accept humbly the gift bestowed on her. She said that Arachne should ask forgiveness from Athene and that Athene was likely to forgive her But Arachne scorned the advice and insisted that nothing would give her greater pleasure than to compete against the goddess. "If I fail," she said, "I will gladly take the punishment, but Athene is afraid to weave with me." Then the old woman threw back her cloak and said, "Athene is here." As Arachne watched, the old woman slowly changed into a beautiful young girl with golden hair. She wore a golden helmet. It was Athene herself. "Come foolish girl," she said, "Athene will try her skill with yours."

In silence, each went to work and for hours their shuttles flew swiftly in and out. Athene used the sky for her loom as usual and, in one hour, she had woven all the gods and their good deeds. In one place you could see the great king Zeus doing unselfish work for others. But Arachne's work had woven pictures of the gods showing all the wrongs they had done. Although her colours were beautiful and the weaving fine, it was full of spite and selfishness. At last the works were finished and Arachne lifted her eyes and looked at the work of the goddess. Instantly she knew that the she had failed and, ashamed and miserable, she tried to hang herself in her web.

But Athene saw her and said in pity, "No, you shall not die. Live and do the thing you are best fitted for. You shall be the mother of a great race of creatures. You and your children and your childrens' children shall be among the greatest spinners on earth." Athene sprinkled Arachne with some juice and immediately Arachne's hair came off and her nose and ears disappeared. Her body shrank till it was no bigger than a fly's and her head grew even smaller. Her fingers stuck to her sides and turned into legs. Athene touched Arachne on the forehead and Arachne became a spider. And from that day to this, Arachne and her family have been clever spinners and still hang by their bodies from their webs.

Write your own myth

Arachne is a myth which offers an explanation as to how a group of animals came into existence; namely spiders. Follow the steps listed below and you can write your own myth to explain how a particular group of animals originated.

☆ Make a list of animals and a particular thing that each can do. For example:

> Birds _ _ _ Sing
> Bees _ _ _ Make honey
> Cats _ _ _ Purr

☆ Choose one of the animals and think of what the animal might have been before it changed.

☆ Think about why it developed its particular skill.

☆ What was its personality like before and after it developed its particular skill?

☆ Perhaps some event or other being caused it to change.

☆ You could give it a special name like Arachne from the myth to match the biological name of the animal. (Spiders are arachnids.)

☆ Does your animal use its particular skill in the same way today?

Instead of writing a myth about a particular skill, you could write a myth explaining how a group of animals developed a particular characteristic. For example:

> Dolphins _ _ _ Friendly
> Sloths _ _ _ _ Lazy

The Chariot of the Sun

EOS, the goddess of dawn, threw open the silver gates of Helios' golden palace which stood high in the east on columns all glittering with gold and studded with precious stones. On the walls, Vulcan had portrayed earth, sea and skies, and on the silver gates were the twelves signs of the zodiac, six on each side. Each morning Helios, the god who drove the chariot of the sun, mounted his golden chariot and drove with great splendour across the sky from east to west.

His golden chariot, glowing like fire, had been a gift from Vulcan. Its axle was the poles, the wheels were of gold, the spokes were of silver and its seat of diamonds reflected the brightness of the sun. Helios wore a golden helmet which sparkled with jewels of all kinds. Brilliant rays of light circled his head, and dazzling beams of light played all around him. His radiance lit up the whole of the sky. So bright was Helios, that only the gods could look straight at him without being blinded.

Helios carefully guided his four fiery steeds with their brilliant golden manes up and across the heavens. The path was steep and narrow and the horses were wild, but Helios held them right on course. At noon he stopped at the top of the sky and looked down at the earth. The land and the sea stretched below; nothing could escape his dazzling gaze. Again Helios drove on and now gave free rein to his steeds.

Far to the west they could see his glittering evening palace and, eager to reach their stables, they descended faster and faster. The shadows grew long and dusk settled over the world as Helios and his fiery team arrived. His five daughters, the Heliades, awaited him him and they unharnessed the tired horses, letting them plunge into the ocean for a cooling bath. Then the horses rested in their stables and Helios talked to his daughters of all that he had seen that day.

In the dark of the night, he boarded a vessel of gold with his team and sailed back around the world on the river Oceanus, which encircled the earth, to his palace in the east. As the way back was shorter by sea than by air, Helios had time to rest in his morning palace before setting out on another day's journey.

Helios had a son named Phaethon, a mortal who lived in Egypt. Phaethon was very proud of his immortal father and watched him pass across the sky every day. Because his father had no time to visit him, Phaethon's friends would not believe Phaethon when he said that Helios was his father. So Phaethon decided to prove to his friends that Helios was his father and one day, after a long trip to Helios' eastern palace, Phaethon begged his father to grant his dearest wish. Helios, who was very fond of his son, promised to grant him whatever he wanted; but when he heard Phaethon's wish he soon regretted this promise.

Phaethon wanted to drive the sun chariot across the sky for one day but Helios knew that no one but he himself could handle the spirited steeds. However, Phaethon would not listen to his father's protests and was determined to have his wish, so Helios finally had to give in. Helios warned Phaethon to hold tight the reins of the steeds and to guide them along the path which had been beaten across the sky for centuries. "If the horses are given their heads," he said, "disaster will follow."

Reluctantly, Helios put his golden rays on his son's head and rubbed divine ointment on his skin so he could withstand the searing heat of the chariot. The impatient steeds, filling the air with their fiery breath, were brought forth as the gates of the palace were thrown open. Phaethon climbed into the chariot and grasped

the reins as the journey began.

Phaethon stood proudly in the glowing chariot. The horses seemed quiet enough as they spurred away into the clear dawn air. The horses tossed their golden manes and drew the chariot up into the heavens. The first light gently touched the tips of the mountains and began to creep into the valleys. As they climbed higher the steeds felt once more the freedom of the skies and they began to sense that unskilled hands were holding the reins. As they passed over Egypt, Phaethon saw that his friends were still asleep and would not see him, so he cracked his whip and turned the steeds off the heavenly path down towards the earth, but nearer than Phaethon had intended.

The horses shied and Phaethon was thrown halfway out of the chariot. Far below he saw the earth spread beneath him and he became pale and his shook with terror and dropped the reins. Without a firm hand to guide them, the horses bolted. The steeds now knew they were in control. They surged towards the earth, seering grasses and trees and setting cities ablaze. Land cracked open, lakes and rivers dried up and seas shrank. The earth was on fire. The steeds then turned upwards and sped so high into the heavens that the earth grew cold and the rivers and seas began to freeze and turn to ice. Phaethon called out to his father but Helios could do nothing. The whole earth was about to perish.

Zeus stood in his lofty temple on Olympus, watching, and shook his head. He had to stop the escaping chariot to save the earth from destruction. So he grabbed one of his thunderbolts and took aim. In a shower of sparks, the chariot flew apart and Phaethon, his body on fire, plunged like a shooting star into the river Po. His sisters cried tears on him, trying to revive him. They mourned so long on the river banks that Zeus took pity on them and changed them into poplar trees, and their tears into drops of amber. And

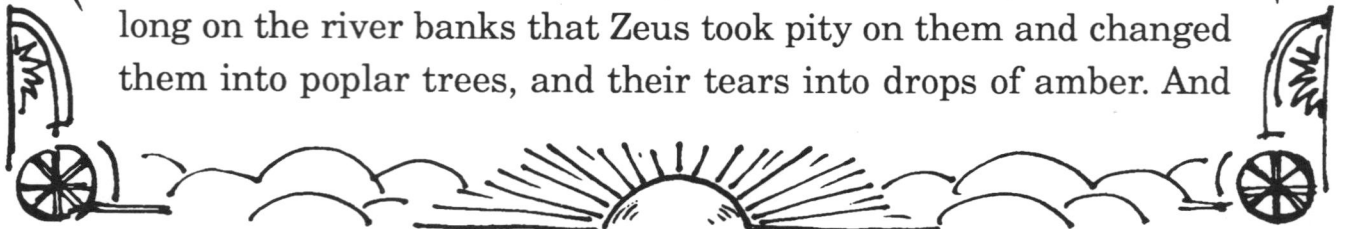

there they still stand, sighing in the wind.

Sadly, Helios set out to find his steeds and chariot. High in the mountains of Ethiopia, the steeds stomped and whinnied in confusion. He threw a cloak over their heads to calm their wild eyes as he led them back, high above their normal path, to their palace in the west.

And for the rest of that day darkness blanketed the earth.

Model of Helios and his Chariot   NAME ....

Read the following extract from the myth *The Chariot of the Sun.*

Each morning Helios, the god who drove the chariot of the sun, mounted his golden chariot and drove with great splendour across the sky from east to west. His golden chariot, glowing like fire, had been a gift from Vulcan. Its axle was the poles, the wheels were of gold, the spokes were of silver and its seat of diamonds reflected the brightness of the sun. Helios wore a golden helmet which sparkled with jewels of all kinds. Brilliant rays of light circled his head, and dazzling beams of light played all around him. His radiance lit up the whole of the sky. So bright was Helios, that only the gods could look straight at him without being blinded.

Helios carefully guided his four fiery steeds with their brilliant golden manes up and across the heavens.

With a partner, create a model to illustrate what Helios looked like riding in his chariot drawn by four fiery steeds.

You will need:
☆ cardboard   ☆ gold and silver foil   ☆ sequins   ☆ paint
☆ glue   ☆ scissors   ☆ coloured paper

Cut out the cardboard to make the characters for your model. Decorate the chariot with the paint, coloured paper and sequins. Create a wonderful costume for Helios out of foil and sequins.

Picture Story
– The Chariot of the Sun

Cut out the following pictures and place them in order to retell the story *The Chariot of the Sun*. You could paste the pictures onto small sheets of paper, back and front, to make a book; or onto a large chart to make a poster; or onto a long strip of paper to make a story strip. Make sure you leave enough room underneath each picture to retell the myth in your own words. Colour the pictures according to the information given in the myth.

King Midas

ONCE upon a time, there was a king who lived in Greece and had almost everything anybody could ever wish for. He had a good wife, a beautiful daughter, much gold and silver, a beautiful garden and servants to wait on him and his family. Yet King Midas was not happy. His only pleasure in life was hoarding gold and yet he never seemed to have enough of it. He loved gold so much that he even named his daughter Marygold. King Midas stored his gold pieces in wooden chests hidden in his cellar and he spent hour after hour every day counting his gold. Before bedtime each night he would open the chests just one more time to look at the gold and touch it.

One day, as King Midas was sitting with his gold, a quivering shadow appeared beside him. The shadow spoke. "You are a wealthy man, Midas, and must be very happy." Midas slowly shook his head. "What!" cried the shadow, "then what would satisfy you?" "Oh," cried the King, without hestitation, "I would like everything I touch to be turned into gold!" The shadow smiled a quiet smile. "Your wish is granted," it said, and faded away.

Midas turned back to his wooden chests and ran his hand over the top of one of them. Instantly, the wooden chest became gold. Midas could not believe his eyes. He ran to his chair and touched it, and it too turned to gold. He sat down excitedly in his golden chair. It was rather hard to sit on, but it was gold. Midas decided to take a walk in the garden before his dinner. He wanted to try his golden touch out on some flowers. He touched a poppy. It turned to gold, stem and all. Midas chuckled with delight. Then he touched a rose and a daisy. Instantly they too turned to gold. Midas could not believe his good fortune.

The servants called Midas to come and eat for they had

prepared a beautiful dinner for their king. There was soup and bread, roast lamb, and a bowl piled high with fresh fruit. "What a lucky man I am," thought Midas, as he began to drink his soup. As soon as he touched the bowl, it turned into gold. And so too did the soup inside. He reached for the lamb and that also turned into gold. He then grabbed some bread in one hand and an apple in the other. But both turned into lumps of gold in his hands. "I'll starve to death," cried the king. He began to think that his golden touch was not as wonderful as he first thought it would be. Full of misery, he sat in his chair made of gold. Just then, Marygold's cat jumped up onto the king's lap. Without a thought, the king began to stroke the soft fur. Immediately, the cat turned to gold, its bristles sharp needles of gold.

"My whole kingdom will be ruined if this continues," thought Midas. As he was deep in thought, Marygold ran into the room searching for her cat. When she saw her cat was gold and cold, she cried. Midas cried too for he loved his daughter and went to comfort her. He touched her shoulder and she froze, turned to gold. Midas was horrified and cried for help. Now the gods had been watching Midas and heard his cry. The shadow appeared again and asked, "King Midas, if you wish to be rid of your golden touch . . ." But Midas interrupted and pleaded. "Anything, anything. I'll do anything." "You must go and wash your hands in the river," said the shadow, "and then bring a pail of water from the river and sprinkle it over everything you have touched."

Midas raced to the river, tripping and falling over in his hurry. On reaching the bank of the river, he fell to his knees and plunged his hands in the water. Then he filled a pail with water and quickly returned to the place where he left Marygold. He dipped his hand into the pail and spinkled water on her. She moved and began to cry for she saw her cat, still frozen gold. Midas then sprinkled the cat with water and instantly the cat came back to life. Midas explained to Marygold what had happened and took her into the garden. He sprinkled the golden flowers with water and they became flowers again. Midas suddenly realised that he was hungry. He had not eaten for some time and so returned to the table. He sprinkled water on the golden lumps and ate with joy. He could hardly believe his dislike for gold.

From that time on, Midas spend most of his time working in his garden. And the smallest flower gave him more pleasure than a hundred pieces of gold.

King Midas Play

Write your own King Midas play using the following guide to help you. In the left hand column make a list of what happened in the story. In the second column write the names of the characters who were involved. In the third column write down in your own words what the characters might have said to one another. The story has been begun for you.

Events: (What happened)	Characters: (People involved)	Dialogue: (What was said)
Rich, unhappy king living in Greece	Midas, wife, daughter	"Oh, I wish I had more gold." – King "We don't need more gold." – Queen "We have a beautiful garden." – Marygold

Work out how many characters you need (and what props you could use) and practise your play before performing it for an audience.

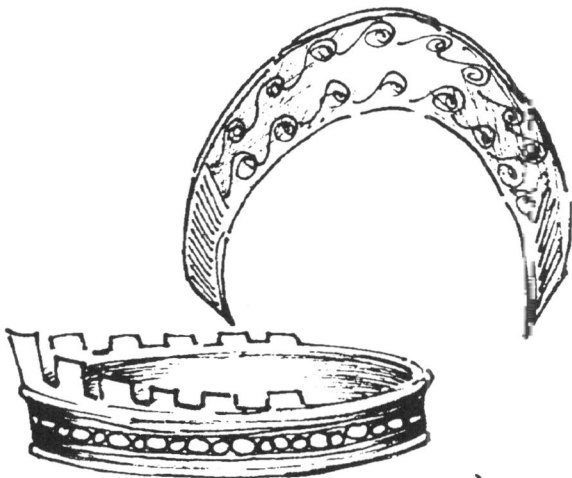

King Midas Diorama

NAME ....

A diorama is a three-dimensional picture in a box. This series of dioramas retells the story of King Midas. Each picture in a box illustrates part of the text.

You will need:
☆ empty boxes (shoe boxes are good) ☆ thin cardboard
☆ coloured pencils or textas or paints ☆ fishing line or thin string
☆ glue ☆ art materials for decorations

Use one box for every scene you wish to illustrate. Stand the empty boxes on their long sides and colour the insides to match the scene. For instance, the top may be blue for the sky, the bottom green for grass; or you may draw an inside scene. Use the art materials (such as felt, cellophane paper, sequins) to decorate the scene.

Cut the thin cardboard into the characters you need for each scene. Make sure they will fit into the box! Colour and decorate the characters. You can either glue the characters to the bottom of the box or suspend them from the top with the fishing line or string to make them stay in position.

When you have finished each diorama, line them up in the right order to tell the story of King Midas. You may like to write a sentence or two for each box, explaining the scene, to glue to the top outside of the box.

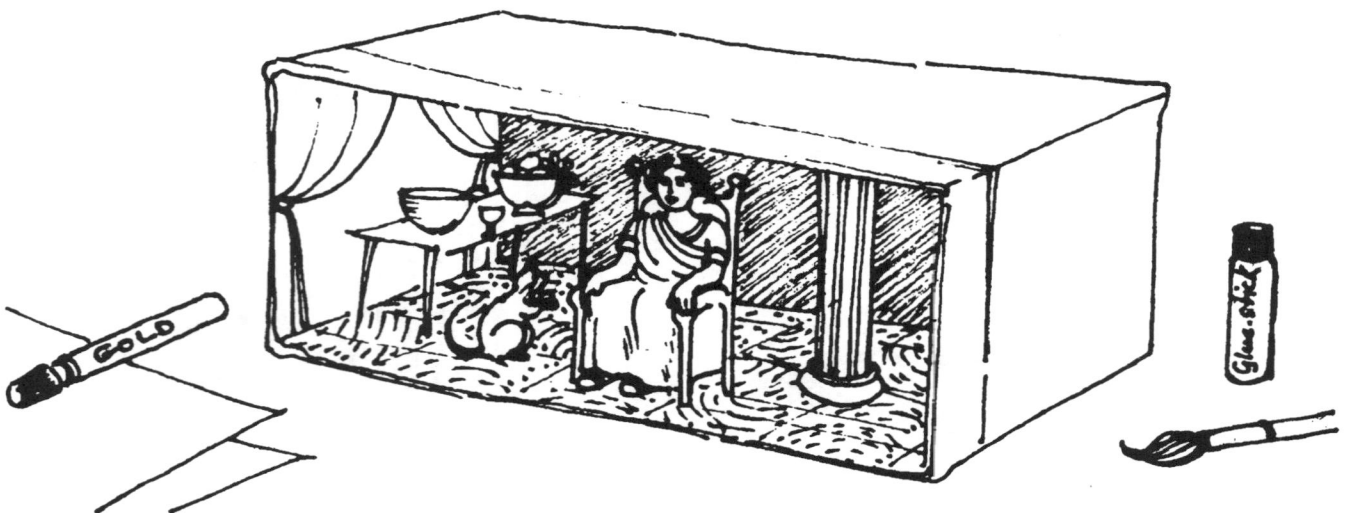

Persephone

*L*ONG, long ago, there was no winter on Earth. There was only spring and summer. There was no bitter cold or snow. Flowers bloomed all the year, trees were laden with fruit and the sun shone, under the care of Demeter, the goddess of the harvest.

Demeter and Zeus had a beautiful daughter, Persephone, who grew up on Mount Olympus. Demeter loved her daughter so dearly she could not bear to have her out of her sight. When Demeter went down to Earth to look after her trees and fields, she took Persephone and they lived on the mountainous island of Sicily. Wherever Persphone danced, flowers sprang up and she became known as the flower maiden.

Persephone was so beautiful that even Hades, the King of the Underworld, fell in love with her. He pleaded with Zeus to give her to him for his queen, but Zeus knew that Demeter would never agree to part with her daughter and so he told Hades that he would have to steal her without Demeter knowing. One day, as Persephone ran about in the meadow gathering lilies and violets, she saw a beautiful flower in the distance and went to pick it. This flower had been planted by Hades himself. As she was standing looking at the flower, she heard a faint sound of galloping horses which seemed to come from far under the ground. Just as she bent to pick the flower, the ground split open right at her feet and up shot a dark chariot drawn by shining black horses. Holding the reins stood dark Hades. He seized Persephone, turned his horses and disappeared under the ground. A herd of pigs eating in the meadow tumbled into the gaping hole after them and Persephone's cries for help faded as the ground closed again just as quickly as it had opened.

Hades, carrying the terrified girl, raced his horses down into the Underworld. Down and down they raced to his dark underground kingdom, Tartarus. In this kingdom, no sun ever shone. Hades carried the weeping Persephone, and sat her beside him on his throne of black marble and crowned her with gold and precious jewels. Persephone was now the Queen of Hades. Dead souls crowded around to look at their new queen. A garden of whispering poplars and weeping willows surrounded the palace of Hades but these bore no flowers or fruit and no birds sang in their branches.

Only one tree in the Kingdom of Hades bore fruit; that was the pomegranate tree. The gardener of the underworld offered the pomegranates to the queen, but Persephone refused to touch them for they were the food of the dead. Silently she walked through the garden at Hades' side and her heart became cold and turned to ice.

Up on Earth in the meadow, the young swineherd stood and wept over the pigs he had lost while Demeter rushed about searching in vain for her daughter. As darkness fell a search party was organised and torches were lit from the fires of the volcano Etna so they could search through the night; but still not a trace of her was found. Demeter searched the world for her lost daughter, and all nature grieved with her. Flowers began to fade and wilt. The leaves on the trees turned brown and fell to the ground, and the fields grew barren and cold. The clouds hid the sun and cold winds blew across the earth; nothing could grow while the goddess wept. The world became cold and sick with hunger.

The gods begged Demeter to again bless the Earth. But she refused to allow anything to grow while her daughter was lost. At last, weary and sad and bent with grief, Demeter turned into a grey old woman. She returned to the meadow in Sicily where Persephone had vanished and asked the sun if he had seen what had happened, but he told her he hadn't, for dark clouds had hidden his face that day. She wandered around the meadow and there she met a youth who was the brother of the swineheard whose pigs had disappeared. He told her that his brother had seen the pigs disappear into the ground and had heard terrified screams of a young girl. Demeter now knew that it had been Hades who had stolen her daughter, and her grief turned to anger. She told Zeus that she would never bless the Earth again if he did not order Hades to return Persephone to her.

Zeus could not let the world perish so he sent his messenger, Hermes, to order Hades to release Persephone. Hades had to obey the orders of Zeus, and sorrowfully he said farewell to his queen. Persephone leapt to her feet but, just as she was about to leave with Hermes, she heard a hollow laugh from the garden. There stood the gardener of Hades, smiling. In his hand was a pomegranate from which there were six seeds missing. He told them that Persephone, not thinking, had eaten the seeds. Neither Zeus nor Hades had power to set her free. The dark Hades smiled. He watched Hermes lead Persephone up to the bright world above but he knew that she must return to him, for she had tasted the food of the dead.

When Persephone arrived on earth, Demeter jumped to her feet with a cry of happiness and rushed to greet her daughter. No longer was she a grey old woman, but a radiant goddess. Once more she blessed her world. The flowers began to bloom, the crops began to ripen and the birds and the animals sang joyfully. "Never again shall we be parted." said Demeter. "Together we shall make all nature bloom." But their joy soon was changed to grief when Persephone told her that she had eaten the food of the dead and must return to Hades. Zeus, in his wisdom, decided that mother and daughter should not be apart forever and he ruled that Persephone return to Hades one month every year for each seed she had eaten.

So each year, when her daughter leaves, Demeter grieves and nothing grows, and winter reigns on Earth. But when Persephone returns, she brings spring and the earth blooms.

Persephone Illustrations

Illustrate the following events from the myth *Persephone*. Paste your illustrations onto separate pages to make a picture story book.

1   Draw a picture to show spring and summer on Earth. There are many flowers blooming, the trees are laden with fruit and the sun is shining. The goddess Demeter is watching over the beautiful Earth. Demeter is wearing a beautiful dress the colour of daffodils and has long brown hair.

2   Draw a picture of Persephone – a beautiful young girl standing on Mount Olympus. Persephone has glistening dark hair and is wearing a dress of many colours. There are flowers all around her and the sun is shining.

3   Draw a picture of Demeter and Persephone looking after the trees and flowers.

4   Draw a picture of Hades, the dark god of the Underworld, sitting on his throne surrounded by the souls of the dead.

5   Draw a picture of Persephone gathering flowers. There is a beautiful flower in the distance.

6   Draw a picture of Persephone picking the flower. The ground has split open at her feet. Some pigs are feeding nearby.

7   Draw a picture of a dark chariot drawn by shining black horses coming out of the Earth. Hades is riding in the chariot.

8   Draw a picture Hades grabbing hold of Persephone and dragging her into the dark chariot drawn by shining black horses. Some of the pigs have fallen into the hole in the Earth.

9   Draw a picture to show the dark god Hades putting a crown of gold and jewels onto Persephone's head to crown her Queen of Hades.

Persephone Illustrations (continued) NAME ....

10 Draw a picture of Tartarus with weeping willows and one pomegranate tree. There are just a few pomegranates hanging from the tree.

11 Draw a picture of a swineheard standing in a field crying. Demeter is running around in the background looking for her daughter.

12 Draw a picture to show flowers fading and dying, leaves on trees turning brown and falling to the ground. The grass is turning brown also. No sun is shining and no birds are singing.

13 Draw a picture of Demeter. She is an old grey woman, bent with grief and is talking to the swineherd.

14 Draw a picture of Demeter. She is angry and is talking to Zeus.

15 Draw a picture of Hermes, a messenger, talking to Hades.

16 Draw a picture of the dark god Hades saying goodbye to Persephone who looks very happy.

17 Draw a picture of the dark Hades and his gardener who is holding a pomegranate. Hades is smiling.

18 Draw a picture of Persephone and Demeter hugging each other. The flowers are beginning to bloom and the sun is shining again.

19 Draw a picture in two parts. One part of the picture shows autumn and winter on earth while the opposite side shows spring and summer.

Pandora's Box

PANDORA was the first woman and had been delicately carved out of marble, her life breathed into her by Aphrodite. All the gods gave her gifts such as beauty and music and Zeus gave her insatiable curiousity. Hermes brought Pandora down from the heavens and gave her to a boy named Epimetheus who had neither father nor mother and welcomed her gladly. One of the first things Pandora saw when she arrived was a box. She asked Epimetheus, "What's in the box?" "It's a secret," replied Epimetheus, "and please do not ask any questions about it. The box has been left with me to keep in safety. I don't know what's in it." "But who gave it to you?" asked Pandora, "and where did it come from?" "I do not know," answered Epimetheus. "That is ridiculous!" exclaimed Pandora. "Just don't think about it," snapped Epimetheus. "Let's go outside for a walk."

They went outside and for a while Pandora forgot all about the box; but when she returned she couldn't help thinking about it again. "Why don't we open it?" asked Pandora, "then we could see for ourselves." "Pandora, what are you thinking of?" exclaimed Epimetheus. He was shocked at the idea of opening the box that had been given to him to take care of. "At least," said she, "you can tell me how it came here." "It was left at the door," replied Epimetheus, "just before you arrived, by a person dressed in an odd kind of cloak." "Oh I know him," said Pandora. "It was he who brought me here. No doubt he intended it for me, and probably it contains pretty dresses for me." "Perhaps," answered Epimetheus, turning away, "but until he comes back and tells us we may, neither of us has any right to open it." And he left the cottage.

Pandora stood gazing at the box. It was made of beautiful dark wood, and was so shiny that Pandora could see her face in it. A beautiful face was carved in the lid and Pandora looked at this face a great many times. At times it seemed to smile at her and at other times it gave a look that frightened her. The box did not have a lock and key, as most boxes have, but it was tied with a golden cord. Pandora said to herself, "Perhaps if I untied the cord, I could tie it up again. There would be no harm in that. I need not open the box, even if the knot is untied."

Just then, by accident, she gave the knot a little twist and the golden cord untwined itself, as if by magic, and there was the box without any fastening. "Oh dear," said Pandora, "what will Epimetheus say when he finds the knot untied? He will know that I have done it." And then a thought came into her head, that since he would think that she had looked in the box anyway, she might as well have a little peep. The face on the lid smiled at her, as if to say there could be no harm in raising the lid. She thought she could hear tiny voices inside the box that whispered, "Let us out dear Pandora, pray let us out!" Pandora could not resist having just one little peep. "There cannot possibly be any harm in just one tiny peep," she said to herself.

Meanwhile Epimetheus, who had been outside, came in. He had stopped to gather some flowers – roses and lilies and orange blossoms – to make a garland for Pandora. When he reached the door he entered softly, for he meant to surprise Pandora. But just as he came in the door, Pandora put her hand to the lid and was about to open the box. If he had cried out, Pandora would probably have let the lid drop. But Epimetheus was really just as curious as she was to find out what was in the box.

There was a loud peal of thunder outside, but Pandora did not hear. She lifted the lid and looked inside. A sudden swarm of winged creatures flew out of the box and brushed past her. Pandora slammed the lid closed but it was too late. She heard Epimetheus cry out, "Oh I am stung! Pandora! What have you done? Why did you open the box?" Pandora let the lid fall and started over to see what had happened to Epimetheus. She heard a loud buzzing, as if a great many huge flies or mosquitoes were flying about. Soon she was able to make out a crowd of ugly little shapes with wings like bats and long stings in their tails. It was one of these that had stung Epimetheus, and before long Pandora began to scream with pain. An ugly little monster had settled on her forehead and was about to sting her, but Epimetheus ran to her and brushed it away.

Little did they know it, but these ugly things were the whole family of earthly troubles. There were evil tempers, all kinds of cares, more than one hundred and fifty sorrows, hundreds of diseases and more kinds of evil than you could talk about. All the sorrows and worries that hurt people today had been locked up in the mysterious box. Epimetheus and Pandora were to have kept it safely locked, so that the people of the world would never be troubled by them.

But now the box was open and the winged troubles flew out of the window and went all over the world. Meanwhile, Pandora and Epimetheus cried bitterly and remained staring at the box. Suddenly there was a gentle tap from inside the box. "What can that be?" said Pandora, raising her head. A soft voice spoke from within. "Only lift the lid and you shall see." "No, no," answered Pandora, "I have had enough of lifting the lid. There are plenty of your ugly brothers and sisters already about the world." "Ah," said the voice again, "they are not brothers or sisters of mine. Come, come, dear Pandora; I am sure you will let me out."

The voice sounded so kind and cheerful that Pandora and Epimetheus together lifted the lid. Out flew a bright smiling fairy-like creature. She flew to Epimetheus and lightly touched the spot where the trouble had stung him, and at once the pain was gone. Then she kissed Pandora on the forehead and her hurt was also cured. "Pray, who are you beautiful creature?" asked Pandora, gazing with wonder at the lovely fairy. "I am called Hope." answered the sunshine figure. "I was packed in the box that I might comfort people when the family of troubles got loose in the world." "And will you stay with us?" asked Epimetheus. "As long as you live," said Hope.

And ever since then, troubles have been flying about the world and making people suffer; but always Hope, the fairy with rainbow wings, comes to bring healing and comfort.

Pandora's Box

NAME ....

Make a model of Pandora's Box.
Paint and decorate a large cardboard box, or cover it with coloured paper.
Line the inside of the box with fabric. Make a list all of the troubles you can
think of. Here are some to get you started:

lying	cheating	cruelty
worry	gossip	jealousy
boredom	greed	selfishness

Draw impish winged creatures like the ones in the story and write the
troubles onto them. Hang the creatures from the open lid of the box as if
they were flying out of the box. Write the word 'Hope' on a card and leave it
in the box as a reminder that there is always hope.

Page 44

Pandora's Troubles

NAME ....

The troubles at the bottom of the page might have been in Pandora's box. Cut them out and paste them under the following headings according to how bad you think they are compared with one another. Compare your list with a friend's.

BAD	TERRIBLE	UNACCEPTABLE

lying	cheating	sickness
cruelty	worry	gossip
unkindness	fighting	jealousy
distrust	boredom	despair
envy	selfishness	sadness
greed	guilt	injustice

Antonyms

The word 'antonym' means 'opposite name'. Each of Pandora's troubles listed below has an antonym. Write in the antonyms next to the troubles.

cheating _____   sickness _____

cruelty_____   unkindness _____

fighting _____   distrust _____

despair _____   selfishness _____

sadness _____   grief _____

greed _____   injustice _____

Adding a prefix or suffix is one way to make an antonym. A prefix is a group of letters which is added to the beginning of a word to change its meaning (a suffix is added to the end of a word). For example:

Word	Prefix/Suffix	Meaning	Antonym
honest	*dis*	*not*	*dishonest*

Make a list of as many words you can think of that use a prefix or a suffix to make an antonym. List them under headings as shown above.

Teacher's Checklist

Names	Can write a story with a beginning, middle and ending.	Can express and explain an opinion about a story.	Can compare and contrast different versions of same story.	Can explain why certain characters acted as they did.	Can explain how particular events affected the outcome of the story.	Is able to summarise the main parts of a text.

Pupil's Own Checklist

Name _____

I have made a book about

_____

I chose this myth/legend because

_____

Some real characters I know from myths/legends are

_____

Some imaginary characters I know from myths/legends are

_____

In the myth/legend of .... I wish
the ending had been different. If only

_____

Responding to Traditional Tales Key Stage Two